LANDMARK TOP TENS

The World's Most Amazing
Castles

Ann Weil

Raintree

Chicago, Illinois

www.heinemannraintree.com
Visit our website to find out
more information about
Heinemann-Raintree books.

To order:
☎ Phone 888-454-2279
▢ Visit www.heinemannraintree.com
to browse our catalog and order online.

© 2012 Raintree
an imprint of Capstone Global Library, LLC
Chicago, Illinois

Customer Service: 888-454-2279
Visit our website at www.heinemannraintree.com

Edited by Megan Cotugno and Laura Knowles
Designed by Victoria Allen
Picture research by Hannah Taylor and Ruth Blair
Original illustrations © Capstone Global Library Ltd (2011)
Production by Camilla Crask
Originated by Capstone Global Library Ltd
Printed in China by CTPS

15 14 13 12
10 9 8 7 6 5 4 3 2

Library of Congress Cataloging-in-Publication Data
Weil, Ann.
 The world's most amazing castles / Ann Weil.—1st ed.
   p. cm.—(Landmark top tens)
 Includes bibliographical references and index.
 ISBN 978-1-4109-4241-8 (hc)—ISBN 978-1-4109-4252-4
(pbk.) 1. Castles—Juvenile literature. I. Title.
 NA7710.W445 2011
 728.8'1—dc22   2010038407

Acknowledgments
The author and publishers are grateful to the following for
permission to reproduce copyright material: Alamy Images
pp. 6 (© Sindre Ellingsen), 9 (© Dieter Wanke), 12 (© Stephen
Saks Photography), 20 (© Alex Segre), 21 (© Porky Pies
Photography), 23 (© Peter Titmuss), 26 and 27 (© dbimages);
Corbis p. 15 (Asian Art & Archaeology, Inc); Photolibrary
pp. 8 (First Light Associated Photographers/Miles Ertman), 10
(P. Narayan), 13 (imagebroker/Jevgenija Pigozne), 17 (Fridmar
Damm), 22 (Hoberman Collection UK); Rex Features pp. 11
(Sipa Press), 18; Shutterstock pp. 5 (© St Nick), 14 (© Martin
Mette), 16 (© Worakit Sirijinda), 19 (© salajean), 24
(© Maugli), 25 (© Konstantin Mironov).

Cover photograph of Schloss Neuschwanstein near Fussen,
Bavaria (Bayern), Germany, reproduced with permission of
Photolibrary (Robert Harding).

We would like to thank Daniel Block for his invaluable help in
the preparation of this book.

Every effort has been made to contact copyright holders of
material reproduced in this book. Any omissions will be
rectified in subsequent printings if notice is given to the
publisher.

Disclaimer
All the internet addresses (URLs) given in this book were valid
at the time of going to press. However, due to the dynamic
nature of the internet, some addresses may have changed, or
sites may have changed or ceased to exist since publication.
While the author and publisher regret any inconvenience this
may cause readers, no responsibility for any such changes can
be accepted by either the author or the publisher.

Contents

Castles 4

Krak des Chevaliers 6

Malbork Castle 8

Arg-é Bam Castle 10

Predjamski Grad 12

Himeji Castle 14

Windsor Castle 16

Castles of Horror! 18

Castillo de San Felipe de Barajas 20

Castle of Good Hope 22

Neuschwanstein Castle 24

Castles in Danger 26

Castles Facts and Figures 28

Glossary 30

Find Out More 31

Index 32

Some words are printed in bold, **like this**. You can find out what they mean in the glossary.

Castles

Nobles began building castles in Europe in the 800s and 900s CE. Many of the first castles were like forts. Wealthy people needed protection from thieves and enemy attacks. Wooden towers, known as keeps, were built on steep hills. This made it easier to see danger from far away. It was also more difficult for enemies to attack when they were going uphill.

Some castles had deep ditches called moats around the outside. Sometimes moats were filled with water. Sometimes they were dry. The people who lived in the castle used a **drawbridge** to cross the moat.

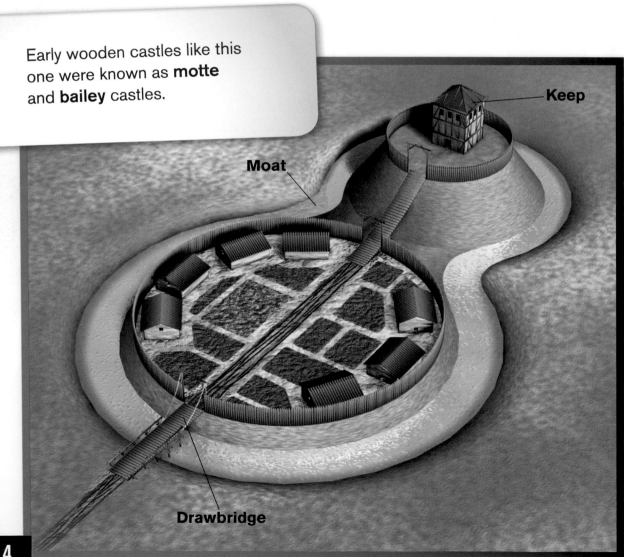

Early wooden castles like this one were known as **motte** and **bailey** castles.

Keep

Moat

Drawbridge

Warwick Castle in England was originally built from wood in 1068. It was rebuilt using stone in 1260.

Wood versus stone

Wooden castles were easy and quick to build. But wood burns, so wooden castles could easily go up in flames. Later, castles were made from stone, with high walls and towers. Some castles had both inner and outer walls to make it even more difficult for enemies to get all the way inside.

Krak des Chevaliers

Krak des Chevaliers means "fortress of the knights." This castle in Syria has stone walls that are almost 10 feet (3 meters) thick. It was built to be able to withstand a **siege** of up to five years. The knights stored extra food inside, just in case. There was also a **well** within the castle so that enemies could not cut off the water supply.

Krak des Chevaliers

Location: Syria, the Middle East

Size: (32,291 square feet) (3,000 square meters)

That's Amazing!
This castle looks much like it did a thousand years ago, when real knights walked through its halls.

Krak des Chevaliers was never attacked, and remains intact to this day.

Krak des Chevaliers was built during the 10th century at a time of religious wars, called the Crusades. **Christian** European **nobles** sent knights and soldiers to the **Middle East**. There they fought against **Muslim** Turks for control of the Holy Land, especially the city of Jerusalem. Many castles were built during this era. They guarded important roads in the area where the Crusades were fought.

Krak des Chevaliers is probaly the most famous of the many castles that were built in the Middle East by the Christian knights during the Crusades.

Malbork Castle

The building of Malbork Castle in Poland started around 1276. This castle was also the home for a group of Crusaders. After the Crusades, these knights ruled the countryside around them for more than 150 years.

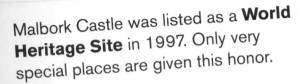

Malbork Castle was listed as a **World Heritage Site** in 1997. Only very special places are given this honor.

Malbork Castle

Location: Malbork, Poland

Size: 1,545,600 square feet (143,591 square meters)

That's Amazing!
It's one of the largest castles in the world!

A Gothic Castle

Malbork is the largest brick Gothic castle in Europe. Gothic refers to a style of **architecture**. Gothic castles have high, curved ceilings. The arches are pointed instead of round. The high walls could fall down if it weren't for the **flying buttresses**, which stick out from the wall and help support the roof.

Time to go!

The knights of Malbork had an unusual way of killing their enemies. They pretended to invite them inside as guests. Then they threw them down the toilet! Medieval castle toilets were built over holes in the outer wall that emptied into a moat.

Arg-é Bam Castle

Arg-é Bam was built around 500 BCE. At that time it was the most impressive building in the region then known as Persia. The **citadel** included food storage buildings, gardens, houses, and **wells**.

Arg-é Bam was surrounded by 20-foot- (6-meter-) high **adobe** walls.

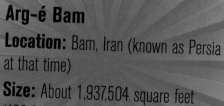

Arg-é Bam

Location: Bam, Iran (known as Persia at that time)

Size: About 1,937,504 square feet (180,000 square meters)

That's Amazing!
This castle is the largest adobe building in the world!

The Silk Road

Arg-é Bam was an important stop along the **Silk Road**. This was not a single road, but many trade routes that connected China and Europe. It cut through the deserts of Central Asia. Traders carrying silk, spices, and other goods traveled together in large groups, called caravans. They hoped this would keep them safe from thieves. Camels were the only animals hardy enough to carry goods along this treacherous route.

In 2003 an earthquake almost completely destroyed Arg-é Bam. Other nations are helping the government of Iran rebuild this amazing castle.

Predjamski Grad

Predjamski Grad means "castle built in front of a cave." The first castle was probably built in Slovenia in the 1100s. It became known as a hideout for thieves and bandits. In the 1400s a knight called Erazem lived in the castle. One of his **ancestors** had built the original castle.

This is one of the three ways into the cave under the castle.

Predjamski Grad

Location: Slovenia, central Europe

Size: About 1,870 feet (570 meters) in length and an average of 427 feet (130 meters) wide

That's Amazing!
This amazing castle is built into the side of a cliff!

The castle we see today was built around 1570. A knights' tournament is held at Predjamski Grad every summer.

Jousting

People from miles around came to watch **jousting**. Knights on horseback charged at each other with large spears, called lances. The idea was to knock your opponent off his horse and win a reward.

Robin Hood

Erazem became known as a local Robin Hood. He and his men used secret tunnels from the caves to smuggle in food when they were under **siege**. Stories say he was betrayed and murdered inside the castle.

Himeji Castle

Himeji Castle in Japan is known as the White **Heron** Castle. The building of this elegant castle began in the 1330s. It was added to many times over the next 300 years. The castle is on top of a steep hill, surrounded by three moats. Its walls are almost 50 feet (15 meters) high. However, Himeji Castle was never attacked.

Himeji Castle

Location: Himeji, Japan

Size: 2,475,00 square yards (230,000 square meters)

That's Amazing!
This castle is said to be haunted by the ghost of a servant girl!

Himeji is the best-preserved castle in Japan.

The ghost of Himeji Castle

There are rumors that the ghost of a servant girl haunts Himeji Castle. In one version of the story, a maid called Okiku broke one of 10 valuable plates. In a rage, the lord of the castle killed her and threw her down the castle **well**. Every night her ghost comes out of the well. She counts from one to nine, and then bursts out crying.

This woodblock print, made in the late 1800s, shows Okiku crying next to the well in which she was thrown.

Windsor Castle

Around 1070 King William I of England built a wooden fort in Windsor. It was built to defend the road to London. Over the years other kings and queens added on new stone buildings. King John fought off two **sieges** from Windsor Castle. Queen Elizabeth I went there to escape the **plague** in London.

What began as a simple wooden fort is now a magnificent stone fortress.

Windsor Castle

Location: United Kingdom

Size: Floor area is 566,280 square feet (52,609 square meters)

That's Amazing!
It's the largest **inhabited** castle in the world.

There are about 1,000 rooms in Windsor Castle.

Windsor Castle Fire

In 1992 the castle was badly damaged by a fire. It started in the Queen's Private Chapel, when a spotlight set a curtain on fire. The flames were finally put out more than 12 hours later.

Windsor Castle today

For more than 900 years Windsor Castle has been a home for British royalty. That's a world record for any castle! Today, it is one of the official homes of Queen Elizabeth II.

Castles of Horror!

Count Dracula and Dr. Victor Frankenstein are fictional characters in novels. But they may have been based on real people and places.

Castle Frankenstein

Did Mary Shelley set her famous novel *Frankenstein*, in the real-life Castle Frankenstein in Germany? It's possible that Shelley might have seen the castle and heard stories of an **alchemist** who lived there in the 1700s. Whether or not it inspired her to write the story, this castle has become associated with her horror novel. Now, it puts on a show full of monsters every Halloween.

Only two towers, a chapel, and some walls remain of this once great castle.

Castle Frankenstein
Location: Hesse, Germany
That's Amazing!
These castle ruins were once the home of real-life barons von Frankenstein.

Dracula's castles?

Romanian prince Vlad the Impaler was the real-life model for Count Dracula. He was famous for torturing thousands of his enemies. Today, many castles in Romania are called "Dracula's Castle." Vlad the Impaler did not own them, but he may have been a prisoner at Hunyad Castle and Bran Castle in Romania.

Hunyad Castle, built during the Middle Ages, looks like a place where a vampire might live!

Castillo de San Felipe de Barajas

Castillo de San Felipe de Barajas is in the port city of Cartagena in Colombia, South America. It defended the city from pirates and other invaders. It began as a small fort on a hilltop. Then in the 16th century the Spanish government that controlled Colombia used slave labor to enlarge it. When it was finished, the fort covered the entire hill. It cost almost 227 tons of gold to build!

It is said that when the king of Spain found out how much the castle cost he said, "For this price, the castle should be visible from here in Madrid!"

Castillo de San Felipe de Barajas

Location: Cartagena, Colombia, South America

Size: The entire hillside!

That's Amazing!
It is the strongest and most expensive Spanish colonial fortress.

The Castillo de San Felipe is famous for its vast network of tunnels.

Talking in tunnels

Underneath Castillo de San Felipe there are miles of tunnels. These were used to bring in food during a **siege**. The tunnels were also carefully designed so that sound waves would carry well. That way, spoken messages could travel long distances. In a time long before cell phones, this was a good way to communicate in the long, dark passageways.

Castle of Good Hope

The Dutch built this fort in the 1600s. At that time the Dutch ruled the southern tip of Africa, as well as island **colonies** in Southeast Asia. They needed a safe harbour in Africa so their ships could stop to take on more food and water for long voyages. They also needed a secure fort to protect themselves and their riches from pirates.

Castle of Good Hope
Location: Cape Town, South Africa
That's Amazing!
The Castle of Good Hope is the oldest surviving building in South Africa.

The castle was built in the shape of a five-pointed star, with cannons at each point.

Pirates!

The Castle of Good Hope was originally built on the beach overlooking the ocean. But over time the ocean washed up enough rock and sand to form an area of land between the castle and the sea shore. The castle is now 1½ miles inland!

The Castle of Good Hope was made a national monument in 1936. Today it is used for military ceremonies and as a military museum.

Neuschwanstein Castle

Neuschwanstein Castle was built for King Ludwig II of Bavaria in the late 1800s. He did not need it for protection. By that time, new castles were designed more like palaces than fortresses.

Neuschwanstein Castle
Location: Bavaria, Germany
Size: About 64,583 square feet (6,000 square meters) floor space
That's Amazing!
It is the most photographed castle in the world!

Does this castle look familiar? The Sleeping Beauty's Castle in Disneyland, theme park was modeled on this real-life fairytale castle in Bavaria, Germany.

The rooms inside the castle are interesting shapes and have beautiful furniture and decorations.

Mad King Ludwig

King Ludwig II did not live to see his masterpiece completed. In 1886, his government declared him insane (mad) and removed him from the throne. Then, with his castle almost finished, Ludwig was found dead. Was he murdered? Did he kill himself? His death remains a mystery.

Neuschwanstein Castle was opened to the public after the death of "Mad King Ludwig." It has been one of the most popular tourist attractions in Germany ever since. More than 50 million people have visited it!

Castles in Danger

Like many old buildings, castles wear away over time. Castles in deserts are **eroded** by sandstorms. Castles in cities are damaged by air pollution. Natural disasters can also put castles in danger. For example, in 2003 an earthquake destroyed Arg-é Bam in Iran.

Time and nature have reduced these amazing desert castles in Uzbekistan to ruins.

Castles today

Some castles are now homes for the very rich, but most are no longer lived in. People do not need castles to defend them against enemy attacks. Even if they did, old castles, such as Krak des Chevaliers, could not withstand modern weapons. Many castles survive today because tourists pay to see them. The money is used for repairs and upkeep, so that people can continue to enjoy these amazing historical buildings.

Castles Facts and Figures

Most castles were built in Europe, but some can be found in Africa, Asia, and the Americas. The first castles were simple wooden forts built for protection. Some castles are huge stone structures still standing today. Others are in ruins, destroyed by humans or nature. Which castle do you think is the most amazing?

Krak des Chevaliers
Location: Syria, the Middle East
Size: 32,291 square feet (3,000 square meters)

That's Amazing!
This castle looks as it did a thousand years ago, when real knights walked through its halls.

Malbork Castle
Location: Malbork, Poland
Size: 1,545,600 square feet (143,591 square meters)

That's Amazing!
It's one of the largest castles in the world!

Arg-é Bam
Location: Bam, Iran (known as Persia at that time)
Size: About 1,937,504 square feet (180,000 square meters)

That's Amazing!
This castle is the largest **adobe** building in the world!

Predjamski Grad
Location: Slovenia
Size: About 1,870 feet (570 meters) in length and an average of 427 feet (130 meters) wide

That's Amazing!
This amazing castle is built into the side of a cliff!

Himeji Castle

Location: Himeji, Japan

Size: 2,475,00 square yards
(230,000 square meters)

That's Amazing!
This castle is said to be haunted by
the ghost of a servant girl!

Windsor Castle

Location: United Kingdom

Size: Flour area is 566,280 square
feet (52,609 square meters)

That's Amazing!
It's the largest **inhabited** castle
in the world.

Castle Frankenstein

Location: Hesse, Germany

That's Amazing!
These castle ruins were once
the home of real-life barons
von Frankenstein.

Castillo de San Felipe de Barajas

Location: Cartagena, Colombia,
South America

Size: The entire hillside!

That's Amazing!
It is the strongest and most expensive
Spanish colonial fortress.

Castle of Good Hope

Location: Cape Town, South Africa

That's Amazing!
The Castle of Good Hope is the oldest
surviving building in South Africa.

Neuschwanstein Castle

Location: Bavaria, Germany

Size: About 64,583 square feet
(6,000 square meters) floor space

That's Amazing!
It is the most photographed castle
in the world!

Glossary

adobe made with sun-dried clay bricks

alchemist person who believed he or she could turn any metal into gold or silver

ancestor grandparents, great-grandparents, and other relatives who lived a long time ago

architecture design and construction of buildings

Christian person who follows the teachings of Jesus Christ

bailey castle's outer wall and courtyard that surrounded the wooden tower, or keep

citadel fortress in a city

colony place that people from another country have occupied and settled in

drawbridge bridge that can be lifted up at one end to stop people from crossing

eroded worn away

flying buttress arched support for a wall

heron wading bird with long legs and neck

inhabited lived in

jousting competition between knights on horseback using lances

Middle East large area that includes the present-day countries of Egypt, Israel, Syria, Turkey, Iran, Iraq, and others

motte large mound of earth upon which a castle was built

Muslim person who is a follower of Islam

noble important, wealthy person

plague very infectious, deadly disease

siege when enemies surround a place to force those inside to surrender

Silk Road ancient trade route from Europe to China

well deep hole dug or drilled to get water

World Heritage Site place with outstanding historical value

Find Out More

Books

Coombs, Rachel. *A Year in a Castle*. Minneapolis, Minn.: Millbrook Press, 2009.

Gravett, Christopher. *Castle.* New York, NY: DK, 2008.

Hicks, Peter. *How Castles Were Built.* New York, NY: Powerkids Press, 2008.

Reid, Struan. *Castle Life.* New York, NY: Powerkids Press, 2008.

Websites

http://www.castles.org
Discover more about some world famous castles.

http://www.historyonthenet.com/Medieval_Life/types_of_castle.htm
This website tells you about all the different kinds of castles.

http://www.historyonthenet.com/Medieval_Life/attacking_a_castle.htm
Find out about how castles were attacked and defended in Medieval times.

Index

adobe walls 10
alchemists 18
Arg-é Bam Castle 10–11, 26
Bran Castle 19
camels 11
Castillo de San Felipe de Barajas 20–21
Castle Frankenstein 18
Castle of Good Hope 22–23
citadel 10
Colombia 20–21
Crusades 7, 8

damaged castles 26
desert castles 26
Dracula 18, 19
drawbridges 4

earthquakes 11, 26
England 5, 16–17

flying buttresses 9
Frankenstein 18

Germany 18, 24–25
ghosts 15
Gothic architecture 9

Himeji Castle 14–15
Hunyad Castle 19

inhabited castles 16, 17, 27
Iran 10–11

Japan 14–15
jousting 13

keeps 4
knights 7, 9, 12, 13

Krak des Chevaliers 6–7, 27

Malbork Castle 8–9
moats 4, 14
motte and bailey castles 4
Muslim Turks 7

Neuschwanstein Castle 24–25
nobles 4, 7

pirates 20, 22, 23
Poland 8–9
Predjamski Grad 12–13

Romania 19

sieges 6, 13, 16, 21
Silk Road 11
slave labor 20
Sleeping Beauty's Castle 24
Slovenia 12–13
South Africa 22–23
Syria 6–7

thieves and bandits 11, 12
toilets 9
trade routes 11
tunnels 13, 21

Uzbekistan 26

Vlad the Impaler 19

Warwick Castle 5
wells 6, 10, 15
Windsor Castle 16–17
wooden castles 4, 5
World Heritage Sites 8